# WALKIES

# WALKIES

Patrick Wright

HEINEMANN : LONDON

*For Terence Frisby*

William Heinemann Ltd
10 Upper Grosvenor Street, London W1X 9PA
LONDON  MELBOURNE  TORONTO
JOHANNESBURG  AUCKLAND

First published in Great Britain 1982
Reprinted 1982, 1983
© Patrick Wright 1982
434 87825 1

Printed and bound in Great Britain by
Redwood Burn Limited, Trowbridge, Wiltshire

# HORRIBLE HABITS.

MAN'S BEST FRIEND.

IN SEASON .

THE AFFAIR.

THE PUPPIES.

ROSEMARY AND HER DOG.

# SHOW DOGS.

THE ADVERTISING CAMPAIGN.

# WALKIES.

EARLY MORNING ALARM.

WALKIES.

THE GREAT DANE AND THE GRIFFON.

# DOG CARE
# AND THAT SORT OF THING.

THE MEDICINE (ONE TABLET FOUR TIMES DAILY.)

ROSEMARY AND HER DOG.

# OBEDIENCE.

OBEDIENCE.

THE KENNEL.

THE ARREST.

THE MASTER OF THE HOUNDS.

George Wright.

# IN THE HOME.

THE SUNDAY LUNCH.

# THE HOMECOMING.

THE LAP DOG.

# ROSEMARY AND HER DOG.

THE APOLOGY.

SUNDAY BLOODY SUNDAY.

GIVING THE DOG A BATH.

THE LAST CHOCOLATE.

D . I . Y .

THE OTHER WOMAN.

# HERO DOGS.

LASSIE.

RIN - TIN - TIN.

THE REGIMENTAL MASCOT.

THE OFFICER OF THE DRUGS SQUAD AND HIS DOG.

SIGNS OF LIFE.
( ONE SMALL STEP FOR MAN.)